Optimize Your Life Series—
Book 3

The Success Habit

Procrastination Hacks to Create Your Best Life One Microburst at a Time

By Stephanie Ewing

Copyright © 2022 by Stephanie Ewing

All rights reserved.

No part of this book may be reproduced in any form by electronic or mechanical means, including information storage and retrieval systems, without written permission from the publisher, except brief passages quoted in a review.

Acknowledgements

To my family, thank you for your patience, love, and support.

I thoroughly enjoy researching, reading and writing about gentle ways to create joy in our lives. Please read and take the nuggets that work for you and create your best life.

Contents

Acknowledgements
Contents
Introduction — 5
Mini Quiz — 7
Chapter 1 - Trick Yourself — 9
Tip One - Fun Apps — 19
Chapter 2 - Starting Small — 20
Chapter 3 - Gaining Momentum — 28
Chapter 4 - Small Wins — 37
Chapter 5 - Be Happy — 46
Chapter 6 - Create Everyday — 55
Tip Two - Great Reads — 67
Chapter 7 - Value of Reading — 70
Chapter 8 - Post-it Notes — 78
Chapter 9 - START — 83
Tip Three - You Got This
Note from the Author

Introduction

Do you struggle with getting things done? Do you feel anxious, nervous, or even a little scared when faced with a large project, task, or goal? Maybe you don't know where to start.

If you fall into any of these categories, you're not alone. I want to help.

The Success Habit: Procrastination Hacks to Create Your Best Life One Microburst at a Time is your lifeline. I'll show you the non-overwhelming ways to kick your butt into gear.

We have a lot of things working against us; it's easy to get stuck in the "Why try?" mentality. But being stuck *really* sucks. This book is your roadmap to attainable success in both tasks and life.

If you're still a little skeptical, don't worry. I was too! I've been able to change my life for the better with these tips and tricks, and I'm a happier, healthier, and more productive person as a result!

Success isn't about being perfect; I think the word 'perfect' is seriously overrated. I'm a mother, and as a parent, I know this firsthand: Success as a parent (or anything for that matter) isn't about being perfect. Perfection is unattainable; do we want our kids thinking that perfect is the only marker of success? Nope. I strive to be a great mother, but I know I can't be a perfect one.

It's not about being perfect: It's about microbursts of success.

My definition of microbursts involve being in the right place, in the right state of mind, and being fully present for those around you. An example of a microburst in parenthood might be your child's first bee sting. That sharp sting, a hiccup of air and sobbing because it hurts so bad. So you scoop your little one into a tight hug and care for them. You grab a piece of ice and numb the sting for a little while.

And at that moment, in that situation, you're the best, most comforting parent in the entire world. After your child stops crying and runs off to play, you smile and acknowledge what you just did and give yourself a pat on the back.

This is just an example, but it illustrates the value of success in microbursts.

Mini Quiz

Before we get started, try this mini-quiz to find your procrastination type. Use what you learn to help motivate you.

Which of these sound like you?

Feeler: I really don't feel like it. I'm too sad, upset, or lonely to get started on that thing I need to do.

Rational: I can't start that now! It's too late and it might keep me awake. Sleep is a biological need. Or, I can't begin until I've done this, nailed that, and finished this.

Busy-Bee: I am working so hard already, how can I possibly tackle anything else?

Inner Critic: I have a negative nelly in my head; my inner critic tells me I'm just lazy or worthless. I'm stupid, and that's why I can't start anything. I probably wouldn't finish it or I would just do it wrong. It's better to just leave it for a better day or for someone else.

Guess what? Each of these procrastination types can achieve microbursts of success.

How you motivate yourself might be slightly different depending on the task, goal, and procrastination type, but this method will work for you regardless.

This book is your how-to guide to accomplishing your tasks, meeting your goals, and doing what you've gotta do with a big smile on your face.

Don't worry—I was skeptical too. I wasn't always a task-driven person, but I've learned the value of ingenuity, starting with the little things, and celebrating what I'm able to get done.

You can do it too, you just need to know how to get your butt in gear!

Chapter 1—Trick Yourself

Procrastination exists on a spectrum, and guess what? You're on it. You might feel you have the best time-management skills in the world, but all of us have things we choose to put off or wait on, whether we'd like to believe it or not.

At one end of what I call the procrastination spectrum, we have the stereotypical "basement boy." He might be in his 30s, doesn't have plans for gainful employment, and lives in his parent's basement. He doesn't want to change, and, to him, his mom's cooking and excellent laundry skills are enough.

There are many serial procrastinator stereotypes, so this is just an example. Serial procrastinators might put off going to the doctor or sending out thank you notes. They might have a difficult time landing a new position at work or reaching out to family members.

It's no way to live.

At the other end are the serial entrepreneurs and time-management junkies; they're in constant motion. They wake up at the crack of dawn and work non-stop until the sun finally sets. They're hyper-motivated and complete tasks. They exercise and have each day planned out to the second on their Google Calendar.

But guess what? They can even put off some important tasks.

Many people fall in the middle; sometimes we forego getting started on a workout plan for a wedding or vacation or maybe you put off grocery shopping or your next dentist appointment. These seem like little things, but wouldn't you be happier if you were good to go and confident in your brand-new swimsuit?

Perhaps some of these resonate with you:

- You might put off laundry until committing arson sounds like a reasonable idea. Why not just burn your old clothes and get new ones, right?

- Do you have large black garbage bags full of unopened mail sitting in your kitchen or hallway? The bags are so large they could bury a small country! But you don't toss them in the garbage or open them.

- Is there an odd lump in your neck or bruise that won't go away, but you put off going to see a doctor?

- Have you told a family member or dear friend you love penguins only to realize you loathe them? People still gift you the knick-knacks, but you refuse to throw them away.

- Maybe your car is well overdue for a maintenance check or an oil change, but it keeps driving just fine so you put it off. It's been three years without a check engine light, so you assume you're good to drive across the country.

- Perhaps you wait until December 23rd to buy your family's holiday gifts. Better late than never, am I right?

These are all procrastination habits, and while these might not resonate with you exactly, there are likely many other things you put off until the last minute.

We're all on the procrastination spectrum. You might procrastinate in ways you didn't even realize, and that's alright! You're human.

It's those nagging little tasks that seem to rear their ugly head at the end of a long day. They're not serving you, and completing them feels pretty good.

The "Lows" of Procrastination

There are different types of procrastinators, and there are many things we procrastinate about, including finances, career advancement, house cleaning, health, relationships, and personal tasks.

Procrastination takes many forms; contrary to popular belief, it's not always waiting until the last minute to dive into a project or putting off asking your boss for a raise. Personally, I procrastinate de-thawing meat and ingredients for dinner! It seems silly and small, but I do it anyway and later regret having to cook nearly-frozen chicken.

These small tasks build up over time. If you wait until the last minute to get your engine checked or put oil in your car, you likely face other (very expensive) maintenance issues. If you wait to go to the doctor to get an odd mole checked out, you risk dire health consequences and/or hefty medical bills.

Again, these might seem like innocuous things to miss, but procrastination is detrimental to your health, and, for some, that's a tough pill to swallow (no pun intended).

Those who identify as serial-procrastinators risk missing out on goals and deadlines. They might experience low-self esteem, frequent distractions, low motivation, depression, and anxiety.

Even those who feel relatively productive experience similar phenomena: they might miss out on job opportunities or promotions, feel anxious in a cluttered home, or suffer from a lack of focus.

That isn't to say a little worry or anxiety isn't a good thing—it is! Good anxiety, otherwise known as eustress, helps us remain motivated. When we set manageable, reasonable deadlines and follow detailed to-do lists, we're much more likely to get things done!

Long story short, procrastination can be dangerous, but if we move toward solving an issue, it's easier to keep on truckin'.

It's physics, but not the difficult kind. Procrastination is simple: an object that's at rest tends to stay at rest. Getting things checked off your to-do list and keeping in forward motion is also like physics. An object in motion tends to stay in motion. So keep moving and work towards conquering your to-do list, and you will build the momentum to do what you *really* love.

Like most things, it's easier said than done. We'll walk through the idea of starting small to get things in motion. It's your job to keep it up.

Tricking Yourself

If you're a self-proclaimed long-term procrastinator, you've likely cultivated many arguments as to why you can't get started and leave things until the last possible moment.

A phrase I often hear is, "I work best under pressure!" and, "Deadlines keep me motivated!" I agree! But here is the thing - you must set your own deadlines and create your own pressure.

Taking the first step isn't easy, and, if it were, no one would be a procrastinator. It's time to trick yourself, but in a good way.

Let's use laundry as an example. Try telling yourself you'll work on the laundry for just a few minutes—no more than ten. Set a timer.

Walk over to the mountain of clothes in the corner, pick out a few pieces you regularly wear, and dump them in the washer with some detergent. Try playing a fun song while you start and dance and sing to the beat.

Meander back over to the Mt. Everest of laundry and spend a few moments sorting your clothes into whites, darks, hand-wash only, etc. Keep dancing along to the rhythm.

When the timer goes off at the ten-minute mark, take a moment to reflect. Think about what you just did. Was it *so* horrible? If it was, give yourself a break and go back to what you were doing before you tackled the clothing mountain. If it wasn't, keep on sorting. Pretty soon, your mountain of laundry will look more like an ant hill.

And finally, you're done. Take a deep breath.

Grab a journal and write down how you feel.
Do you feel accomplished?
Do you feel clean and ready to tackle the next task?
Maybe you feel a little tired or sluggish—you've been putting the task off for a reason.

After jotting down a few notes about how you feel, read over what you've written. Consider how you feel about what's on the page. Do you feel good about it? Or do you feel a little embarrassed? Don't worry, you're the only one reading your procrastination journal!

Next, write down some affirmations. Affirmations are written in the present, not the past or future. Use "am," and not "did" or "will." If you make the future the present, you're already ahead of the game.

In this example, write something like, "I am a laundry ninja," or, "I'm a laundry-doing pro." Then, write about what you will do, but again, in the present. You might write, "I know I am a successful person," and "I am a taskmaster."

You might feel a little silly writing these down, but affirmations get you thinking about what you can do, and I bet you can do a lot! Get yourself thinking about how you can use affirmations to your advantage.

Tricking yourself can take on many forms. In this example, you set a timer, and told yourself *only a few minutes* but the same concept applies to many goals and tasks.

Another trick is rewarding yourself. Maybe you've been forgetting (or neglecting) to call a friend or family member. The reason doesn't matter, but you know you should. Relationships are important.

You tell yourself, "I'm calling this person at 2 pm today" and prepare a mini-reward. Your reward can be anything: watching a bit of a TV show, a hot cup of hot chocolate, or even a short TikTok break.

2 pm rolls around and you give them a short call. You say, "Hey, just thinking about you and I wanted to check in—how are you today?" They might pick up, or they might not. Regardless, leave a message and congratulate yourself - you did something worth celebrating.

The Procrastination Hack: Does it Really Work?

The short answer: Yes, absolutely! Tricking yourself seems like a pretty small or even silly way to kick your butt into gear, but there's nothing silly about changing your life. It's high time, my friend.

We can't expect our lives to change on a dime if we keep everything the same. I think that is the definition of insanity!

Consider what procrastination is doing to your life. Does it make you happy? Do you feel satisfied and fulfilled? I can say this without a doubt: When I am procrastinating about a big task, I feel pretty crappy.

Look at yourself in the mirror and take time to think about what you've been putting off. Keep reading, and soon, you'll be able to venture closer and closer to your desired finish line.

Tip One
Fun Apps

Get a daily dose of positivity with the "I am" affirmation app.

Calm is a great app for sleep and meditation. Join the millions experiencing better sleep, lower stress, and less anxiety.

Meditation app with the world's largest free library of guided meditations.

Chapter 2—Starting Small

Have you ever neglected a task or put off something because you felt it was too complicated? Did you feel the task was over your head or contained too many moving parts? I certainly have.

Some tasks or goals are a culmination of many smaller ones. For example, think about writing a book—I'm no stranger to this one. Running a half-marathon and training for one is another.

Both goals contain many steps: Books take months (if not years) to write, and most experts say it takes up to 20 weeks for a non-runner to prepare for a marathon.

If you measure the complexity of the task by the end result—as many of us do—it becomes incredibly complicated. No one begins learning something by thinking, "I should know everything and anything there is to know before I can begin." If that's how you feel, it's time to change your mindset.

Learning is an incremental process—we take baby steps before we take large strides. Think back to middle and high school: You couldn't do Geometry overnight! It took years of addition and subtraction to get you an A in Geometry or Trig class!

Taking things one step at a time is how we accomplish any task—no matter how big or how small.

Let's break it down together.

Checking Your Language

Think about your language. How we speak and why we speak reflects who we are and how we feel; changing it is a small way to alter your outlook.

For example, let's say you're a part of a book club, and you really need to finish the book before your group meets next Friday. You're excited about the book club (well, mostly the cheese and wine part), but you've been dragging on your reading progress.

You look at the book on your shelf; it's screaming "Read me!" but you can't bring yourself to get started. You think, "How on Earth am I going to read over 200 pages in like…10 days?! Ugh, I'm such a failure."

Think about your wording: Words like "how am I" and "failure," along with exaggerated numbers aren't helping you think more positively about the goal.

Let's rephrase.

Instead, you think, "Hmm, I need to get started on this book. I have ten days and 200 pages. How do I break this up and enjoy it?"

The second sentence sounds much better than the first—you're being kind to yourself and giving yourself the space to think logically. Emotion-charged words are great in small doses, but they aren't helping you prepare for Friday's book club.

Let's try another example. You're looking in the mirror after a shower and you're not too happy. You have a beach vacation next month, and you *really* want to feel confident in your new swimsuit! There's no shame in that.

You look into the mirror and think, "Ugh, I have so far to go. I don't look or feel ready at all!"

That wasn't so productive, was it?

Instead, think, "Hmm, I'm not happy with where I am, but I have a little time. How can I get started to accomplish my goal?"

That sounded much better, right? Use language to call yourself to action. Beating yourself up over a task or step isn't helping anyone, especially not you. When we're hard on ourselves and think negatively, we're less likely to start an action toward our goal.

Change your self-talk; you'll enjoy yourself more and get more accomplished.

The Small(er) Steps

This might sound easy, or even a little silly, but there's value in reviewing the basics. Time and task management are tricky, even for time management/productivity junkies!

We'll use a few examples to help you understand what needs to be done, but again, these are just examples, so feel free to swap them for whatever's been on your mind lately!

In this section, we'll break down how to reduce large tasks into smaller, more manageable ones.

Step One

Define what it is you're trying to do. This might seem like a relatively simple step, and, in theory, it is.

Consider what the task is and write it down. Try to use one sentence. For example, "I want to write a novella" is much easier to swallow than, "I want to write an epic science fiction trilogy set in a distant galaxy." Sometimes just taking the time to define the task will make the process much more manageable.

After you've defined the task, consider what it truly is: Is it a goal, project, task, or accomplishment? In the writing-a-book example, you're working towards a goal. A project would be something like compiling old photos, reorganizing your closet, or finishing a proposal for work. A task is something smaller, though no less important; a task would be something like taking out the trash, doing laundry, or running a particularly boring errand. Lastly, an accomplishment would be something like getting admitted to graduate school, getting a new job, etc.

So what is it you're trying to do? Add that in a separate sentence to what you've written.

Step Two

Begin planning how you'll work through the task, project, or accomplishment.

Craft your to-do list. You can use a Word or Google Document and write down the necessary steps you'll need to take to accomplish your goal. You can also use old-fashioned pen and paper; it's up to you!

Use bullet points or checkboxes to mark each one. Don't be afraid to make the things you must "to-do" as small as you'd like. Each step should be measurable and manageable.

If you're trying cooking, think back to the cooking example I used earlier. Open up a document and begin writing "Google basic cooking skills," or, "call Mom to ask for a little cooking lesson."

Move on to jotting down other things you'll need to do, like "buy a beginner's cookbook," "research easy recipes," "schedule cooking class," or, "buy basic ingredients."

In the marathon example, you might look up training guides and use those to plan your next steps. You might write, "buy running shoes," "walk three miles," "walk two, run one," etc.

The tasks should be larger towards the end of the list, so you might say, "Make pasta with an easy homemade red sauce recipe," or "Run a 10k" near the end of the list.

Step Three

Create your own deadlines. Again, these should be reasonable. If you're training for a marathon, it wouldn't be a great idea to set your goal for two weeks from now if you haven't run in years!

For me, if I'm procrastinating something at home, like cleaning, organizing, or laundry, a manageable deadline would be something like inviting someone over for dinner for a little adult dinner party.

Now you not only have the desire to finish your project, but you have someone to verify your progress. You just created a fun and realistic deadline.

Don't set your deadline too soon; if you've never cracked an egg, perhaps give yourself a week or two to become a Gordon Ramsey cooking pro before you ask your friends over for homemade medallions of beef with cabernet reduction.

Step Four

Take the tiniest first step on your to-do list. You might need to purchase what you'll need to get started or try some research.

If you need to schedule an appointment, make the call! It'll take less than 10 minutes. If the task requires some Googling, whip out your phone or laptop.

If we're using the cooking example, the first task might be checking out some "How to Cook" books, articles, or sites. You might call your mother (they make a mean lasagne) and ask for a quick lesson. Maybe order a cheap beginner's cookbook on Amazon.

If your goal is getting accepted to graduate school, begin researching what you'll need to get started with the process. Your first steps might be "Buy a GRE or GMAT study book," "Make a pros and cons list" to narrow down your options, etc.

Each of these takes just a few minutes, and you'll feel much better about the process.

Slow & Steady Wins the Race

Baby steps might seem a little silly; most people use the "tortoise and the hare" adage when discussing how to complete tasks, but that's much easier said than done.

Realistically, breaking larger accomplishments down into smaller ones is a great way to get started on your goals. Follow the to-do list tip, create manageable goals, and enjoy hitting them with ease!

Chapter 3—Gaining Momentum

As we discussed in the first chapter, an object in motion stays in motion. That's why it's important to get moving! Nothing is stopping you from getting started but yourself. More often than not, we're our own worst enemies.

Consider the Goal

What is it you want to accomplish? Think about what you want from life. Try journaling or doing a bit of research. What piques your interest? How might you accomplish this interest?

Next, consider *why* you're interested in this concept or accomplishment. Do you want to share your story? If you're thinking of a triathlon, why do you want to make it past the finish line?

I didn't always know I wanted to write a book, but over time and with a lot of self-reflection, I realized this was a true goal of mine. I wanted to share what I've learned with the rest of the world!

I discovered Gundi Gabrielle's book, *Publishing: Self-Publish a Book in 30 Days! The Proven 4-Week Formula to go from Zero to Bestseller &*

#ShareYourAWESOME with the World!, and found my motivation.

Writing a book may or may not be in your future, and that's alright. Any task, project, or goal, large or small, can be tackled in the same way. Know where and how to begin.

Write down why you want to tackle the goal. Use what you've written to guide you and keep you motivated throughout the process.

Counting Down to Takeoff

Have you ever heard of Mel Robbins's trick of counting down? It's not too hard or complicated, I promise!

Mel Robbins came up with the count-down method while watching a rocket launch. She calls it the "five-second rule," but it doesn't refer to when you drop a bagel on the ground.

Give yourself five seconds to get started on a task. Let out a deep breath and start at five. Slowly count backward until you get to one. When you've finished counting, move! If you don't move after the five-second window, your brain will backtrack, and you won't do the task at all!

It's about intent. When we intend to do something, it creates a sense of urgency. All of a sudden, your brain *needs* to do it.

It's the same as disciplining children—do you remember when your parent or guardian used to count down from five or ten before you were to do what they asked? My mother was a huge fan of this tactic. I was instantly pressured to do what she was asking!

So count down from five, get up, and do what you've gotta do!

Think about the task. Maybe you've been putting off laundry or washing some dishes. The task itself doesn't matter, so substitute what you need to do to feel accomplished.

If you've been putting off laundry, you might think, "Oh look! I already have clothes in the washer!" Countdown from five and get up to move them to the dryer. When you hear the final "ding," countdown from five and get folding.

Maybe you've been considering getting started on a workout regimen; it's been months (or maybe longer) since you've hit the gym. You want to get started (you have your sister's wedding in a few months, and you want to feel confident in photos), but you've been lagging!

Countdown from five, stand up, and do a few squats! Try no more than five or ten. Maybe do a short plank. What you do is totally up to you!

Here's the best part—after five squats and a brief break, you'll feel much more accomplished. You might think, "Well great! Look at me doing some exercises! Why not do a few more!" So you count down, stand up, and repeat the process.

Soon, you'll become bored with the process; after a few counts and mini-workout rounds, you might think, "Hmm, it might be time to break out my old tennis shoes and go for a walk!"

Take a small break to think; consider the task or thing you're dreading. What do you need to do to get there, and why are you so opposed to getting started?

You might be concerned about some of these:

- Are you putting off paying the electric, gas bills, or rent?

- Are you nervous about creating a monthly budget (you're certainly not alone with this one)?
- Are you apprehensive to re-do your resume or hop online to go job hunting?
- Are you putting off cleaning your kitchen, closet, or living room?
- Maybe you're nervous about getting back out on the dating scene. You've heard Tinder horror stories, but you'd love to meet someone!

If so, that's okay! If these don't resonate with you, there are likely other things that will. You're human, and we all have things we're looking to put off; everyone has mixed feelings about the first step.

The task you need to start with is the one you've been neglecting or the one that makes you roll your eyes.

Breathing, counting to five and getting started with a small step makes you feel empowered. Use that empowerment to begin the next step on your list.

Just Take One Bite

My mother used to say, "just take one bite," and while I never really understood why as a child, I've gained an understanding of what she was trying to say: Just take one bite means doing something you don't want to do, the task you think you will loathe. Just get started - it might not be as bad as you think!

For example, I don't like picking out my clothes for the day. It seems silly and a little stupid, but it's my tough task! I find it cumbersome, anxiety-inducing, and annoying. I check the weather multiple times before heading to the closet (what if it rains?) and pick through options I either don't like or find boring. You never know who you'll see or meet one day, right?

I used to put off picking out clothes until the rest of my day was ready: I'd make coffee, eat breakfast, get showered, go over my planner, etc, all before getting dressed!

But I know I don't like picking out clothes, that's not a secret. So I started by just taking one bite. Now I start with my pants.

I pick out my pants for the day before doing anything else—I get out of the shower, do a few squats, and walk over to the closet. I check the weather beforehand (some things never change), and pick out the pants I feel comfortable in. After that, choosing a top and shoes feels much less complicated. Not *so* hard right?

Everyone has a food dish they'd prefer not to eat. I often put off grocery shopping, trips to the dry cleaner, or exercising. We make excuses for not starting—maybe it's raining out, you're much too busy to get started sorting clothes, or maybe you say gym memberships are too expensive.

We all love excuses, but it's those excuses that are stopping you from accomplishing what you want.

Start the day with what you don't want to do. Not only will you get it out of the way, but finishing an arduous task before you move on to others you enjoy gives you a sense of accomplishment. You've already done the hard part!

Maintaining Motivation

Experts argue this is the hardest step. You've counted down, and gotten started, so what comes next?

It's the middle part that seems to be the real kicker.

That's why we check our progress. Think back to the to-do list you created. To-do lists aren't just for starting tasks—they help us finish and maintain them too!

Sometimes I don't have the motivation to write, and I've met other writers who feel similarly. Writers might come up with a great idea, do their research, create an outline, and tackle the first page, only to look at a blank page when they come to the second one.

In these instances, I check the word count. And, I check it often. I look at how many words I've gained every few minutes and use the number to push me toward my goal. I think, "Oh look! I've added a few hundred words to the chapter. I guess that wasn't *so* bad—I'll write a few hundred more!"

I feel a wave of motivation at the end of my writing session. Had I not checked the word count, I would still be at nearly zero. But I did, and I'm already halfway through! I feel accomplished and ready to tackle what's next.

Accomplishment is our body's way of rewarding us. It's like a piece of candy you give to a child after they put away their toys. Our brains release important hormones and chemicals when we finish a task, especially one we've been neglecting. We feel invincible!

Train your brain to give you more of what you want, and do it naturally. The reward is more than worth it!

Remember to reward yourself for your progress, no matter how small. You got out of bed today—that's a win! Did you go to the gym? Awesome! These are small steps, and small steps become big ones. Buy a calendar and put a huge checkmark on the days you go to the gym. Just the act of adding that mark will release some of the awesome brain chemicals.

Soon, you'll be able to use your momentum to accomplish the impossible. It's well within your reach.

Chapter 4—Small Wins

You're an object in motion, but what comes next? What happens after you get the ball rolling? How can you maintain that mindset?

Breaking the procrastination habit isn't easy; it takes time, effort, and consistent check-ins. Oftentimes you'll feel good for a while: You'll complete tasks with ease (you're an object in motion after all!), but over time, your motivation dwindles and you lose sight of the goal.

In this Chapter, we'll discuss small wins, or celebrating the little things. You can do it, you just need to follow the process.

Beauty in the Little Things

We tend to demotivate ourselves by looking ahead to the next step. I fall into this category quite often. I'll find myself working on a chapter of a book, conducting my research, and typing away, only to keep thinking about the grocery shopping that needs to be done, or the editing the chapter needs. It's exhausting and tiring. I often feel like no matter how productive or task-oriented I become, I'm still a failure.

It's not just about breaking down tasks—it's about *focusing* on the small tasks. We become overwhelmed when we overthink it. Breaking down the task of laundry is relatively simple: You've gotta sort the clothes, carry them to the washer, add detergent, and so on. But focusing on those tasks and remaining mindful is a whole other bear.

Let's say you're breaking down the task of cleaning out your closet. You've decided to look at one shelf or section at a time. You take everything off your shelf and place it on your bed. You grab a few trash bags to sort the clothes and mark them "Donate" and "Keep." You pick up each item and evaluate it: Should it stay, or go? Soon, you've finished one shelf!

That's only part of the process. You might find your mind wandering to the other shelves while you sort the first one: They're full of clothes that need to be sorted, and soon, you become overwhelmed. You start to think, "There's just too much to do!!!"

But there isn't, because you've broken down the tasks. You decided to sort and organize one at a time, and that's what you did. If there are four shelves in the closet, you're 25% done! Look at the shelf—it looks nice and organized and is ready to go! Pat yourself on the back.

Measure your success by what you've already done. You can only control the now.

Focusing on the 'Now'

As I said, maintaining motivation is difficult. Again, if it were easy, you'd already be a procrastination-busting pro!

I was scrolling through social media the other day and came across a post from a friend; they documented their entire day, step by step. The post read:

*"I showered,
made food,
did the dishes,
took out the trash,
and watched a few videos.
Look at me adulting!"*

If everyone talked about their day's accompaniments like my friend did, we'd all feel pretty damn good. He's celebrating what he *did* without considering what he didn't.

But again, this is much easier said than done. At the end of a long day, most of us focus on what we didn't do. You might lie in bed and think, "I showered tonight, cooked dinner, did the dishes (finally!), took out the trash in the kitchen and bathroom, and watched some cool videos. Okay. But I didn't finish that big project for work, I didn't work on my crafting, I didn't do my laundry, and I didn't go to the gym like I'd wanted to. I'm a failure."

That doesn't sound too good, right? But unfortunately, most of us feel this way at some point in our lives (or every day, even though we don't like to admit it). You can't walk through life feeling as though you're wasting time. You're not a #loser or a #nolifer. You're a #badassperson doing the best you can. And that's something worth celebrating.

It's about how we talk to ourselves and interpret our actions. We discussed the power of language in the earlier chapters, but the same concept applies here.

Affirmations and Mental Health: The 'Now' Hack

So how do you fix your mindset? The work you need to do is in your own head, meaning you're in control. Yet again, it's much easier said than done. That's why we use affirmations and personal mantras; use language and mental tools to effectively conquer negative thoughts.

Affirmations work. I can tell you this firsthand. I never thought I'd have the skills or tools (or thoughts) to become an author. I'd think to myself, "What do I have to say?" or, "How could I write an entire book?"

It wasn't until I conquered my negative thoughts and procrastination-based mindset that I opened my eyes to what's possible. It turns out that I had a lot to say! And with enough effort and research, I CAN write.

Affirmations and mindfulness involve no equipment, no money, little effort, and little time, making them perfect for chronic procrastinators! It's a free way to conquer your thoughts and reclaim your life.

Sit down in a comfy place, whether it be your bed, your desk, your living room, the library, etc! Surround yourself with things that make you feel cozy. I'm a pillow person myself (I love soft objects), so I sit in my bed with my lap desk and write out my affirmations.

After a few deep breaths, I state my affirmations aloud in a clear, calm voice. Focus on how you sound. Slow your pace and consider how you can state your affirmations more confidently.

Mindfulness is much the same. It's the practice of being present in the moment without jumping to the next. Intrusive, negative thoughts occur when we let our minds wander. Mindfulness involves focusing on what you're doing, what you're feeling, and where you are at that exact moment.

Let's say you're cooking dinner. You've made the recipe many times, more times than you can count. You don't have to think about ingredients, the process, or cooking times. You let your mind wander while you cook. You might think, "What do you have to do later today? What's next on the agenda? How do I feel about what happened today?"

It's the wandering that's the problem. Instead of letting your mind roam to places it doesn't need to go, focus on what you're doing. Say, "I'm cutting the chicken and putting it in the oven. I'm re-reading the recipe. I'm measuring the spices and adding them to the sauce on the stove."

Mindfulness is a powerful way to remain fully alert without becoming overly reactive or stressed. We can only control what's right in front of us.

Don't just take my word for it. Mindfulness, affirmations, and deep breathing have years of scientific research to back their validity. Many forms of therapy, like Cognitive Behavioral Therapy (CBT) and Dialectical Behavioral Therapy (DBT) use mindfulness and deep breathing to help people focus on what they can control without jumping to what they can't.

If you spend a few minutes or thirty seconds a day practicing affirmations and incorporating mindful moments throughout the day, you might see improvements in mood, and memory, fewer intrusive thoughts, lower blood pressure, and a better overall outlook!

Therapy: To Try or Not to Try

If you've tried affirmations, mindfulness, small tasks, and everything in between but you're still beating yourself up or experiencing thoughts that don't serve you, it might be time to try therapy. There's no shame in therapy; it's a tool to help yourself reach your goals.

Do some people need therapy to improve their mindset? Yes, I think so. If you feel you fall into this category, you're not alone. Would all of us benefit from therapy, or just having someone to talk to? Again, probably!

Some serial procrastinators procrastinate about therapy. I'll admit, making the first call isn't always easy. If you feel this applies to you, break the process into smaller or more manageable steps.

Look online for nearby therapists or check your insurance's site for local recommendations. Make sure the therapist or professional you choose specializes in what you're struggling with. Many communities and therapists offer discounted or subsidized rates, so make sure you explore all your options!

If you're in a crisis, call for immediate help. You can call 911 or 988 for the National Suicide Prevention Lifeline for those living in the United States. There are other text-based services available for a short-term stop-gap. Try texting the National Crisis Textline for short-term crises.

I'm not a medical professional or a therapist—think of me as an encouraging friend. I want to make sure you have the options and information you need to successfully achieve your goals.

Small Things & Big Things

Maintaining your mindset, focusing on the present, and prioritizing affirmations aren't easy. These are skills that take time to learn and develop. You weren't great at cooking scrambled eggs the first time you tried it (maybe you used too much butter or ended up with eggshells in your breakfast), but over time, you've learned how to make a delicious and hearty meal with ease. (For pro-status scrambled eggs add some cream cheese.)

Focus on what you're doing in the context of what you *can* do. You can only conquer what's real and what's in front of you. There's no sense in beating yourself up over what you haven't gotten to quite yet!

With enough practice, forethought, and knowledge, you'll be your own #smalltaskboss!

Chapter 5—Be Happy

Easier said than done, right?

We all strive for happiness. We look for it in money, material goods, people, relationships, and professional achievements. Stability is important, but even those with a nice house, clean yard, lovely family, and thriving career experience bouts of unhappiness. So why is that?

Money Doesn't Buy Happiness, Right?

You've heard this phrase before, likely more times than you can count. Does money really buy happiness?

Not exactly. Only one-fifth of Americans believe money can buy happiness. The other four-fifths know that money only plays a small role in what it means to be satisfied.

Money buys stability; it brings financial wellness, opportunities, and material goods. I love a great meal at a nice restaurant, but I know I don't need one all the time! A nice five-bedroom house is great, but it won't quell intrusive thoughts or negative events.

Experts say money buys happiness to a certain extent, but once one reaches the lower-middle class, money doesn't seem to make as much of a difference in overall life satisfaction. Other experts say that when one defines their own satisfaction in terms of dollar signs, they're much less likely to be happy.

The happiest people I know are the ones who don't focus on money. My happiest friends focus on family, friends, tasks, and the little things. There's no need to run yourself ragged for what you deem "success." Work hard on what you are passionate about, then it won't seem like work.

If money and finances are a concern, try budgeting! Budgeting completely changed my life, and it can change yours too. There are many free resources for those looking to try a budget, so give it a shot! Budgets are a reflection of what you do have, not what you don't. They're a great way to measure progress, growth, and spending.

So no, money doesn't buy happiness, but that doesn't mean it's not a factor. I'm by no means saying you should sit down and completely rethink your income. I'm asking you to focus on what's in front of you.

But what comes after money? How do you focus on what you do have? Let's talk about it!

Happiness & Satisfaction: Are They Related?

I certainly think so. The word happy is synonymous with contentment, or the state of feeling at ease with one's life.

Experts believe in what's called a happiness bell curve. When we're in our early lives, our needs are, for the most part, taken care of. We focus on school, part-time jobs, friends, etc. Until our teens, our stress comes from ourselves and our accomplishments. You might remember feeling stressed about homework, a family member, or some tricky drama with your high-school partner, but now you might look back and think, "Hmm, I guess that really wasn't too stressful at all."

Our stress levels heighten in our twenties and thirties. Maybe your boss is on your back about a proposal or deadline or you and your partner are in the midst of taking care of a young child. As we enter our forties, family stress tends to intensify, children need to be picked up from extracurriculars, and work becomes more arduous and anxiety-inducing.

Yet, as we enter our fifties and sixties, our stress levels decline. Many people enter retirement and their children move out; errands become less frequent, and life seems overall easier.

This phenomenon doesn't apply to everyone, but in general, stress and unhappiness follow a bell curve, peaking in our forties and dropping off in our fifties and sixties.

Improving Your Outlook

Life hands us reasons not to be happy. You might get passed over for a promotion or opportunity or experience a personal loss. You might feel upset about a difficult relationship or family matter. That's okay. It would be crazy to believe we can be blindly happy in the face of emotional and personal turmoil. That's ludicrous.

Do you know what's *not* crazy? Changing your outlook.

Shifting your perspective won't stop negative events from happening, but it might help improve your reactions. Happy people don't fly into a blind rage on the freeway, nor do they yell at the woman at the checkout line when the store is out of their favorite cereal. They react positively, and it's infectious.

So how is it done?

Consider the word control. What do you have control over? You can control your mind, your thoughts, your habits, and your reactions. You can't control the actions of others, even though you might want to.

Learning to let go of what you can't control and embracing what you can is key to happiness. And, when you sit down and think about it, you'll realize you can control much more than you think!

Let's say your partner has a negative reaction to the meal you cooked for dinner or they're upset about an unfinished task. They might use harsh words or raise their voice, and that's not your fault. They're human, just like you! You can't control them.

You *can* control your reactions. Instead of matching their negative energy, you can use calm words or separate yourself from the situation.

Perhaps your boss passed you over for a large project at work. There are likely many factors at play: budget, workload, personal bias, and other information you aren't aware of. It's not your fault!

You can control how you react. Instead of flying off the handle, you can work harder, ask for opportunities, and speak up for yourself.

Negative events are a part of life. When you experience a negative event, no matter how small or mundane, take a step back. Ask yourself these questions: What other factors might be at play? How does this fit into the bigger picture? In five years, how will I feel about this event?

You can let negativity infect you, or you can choose to focus on yourself and improve. I'd choose the latter.

How to Be Happier

I've said this many times, and I'll say it again—it's much easier said than done. Happiness isn't like a light switch—we can't turn it on and suddenly find satisfaction. However, we can make little changes to strive toward happiness. Little changes become big ones.

Firstly, avoid comparing yourself to others. There will always be people you deem smarter, fitter, thinner, healthier, wealthier, or more successful than you. There are people everywhere who seem "better" than you. Newsflash—it's likely a facade.

Think of yourself, for example. Let's say you're headed to a nice dinner with a few friends you admire. Maybe they work out daily, have a beautiful family, or hold "successful" jobs. They have struggles too. They're human!

We don't broadcast the parts of our lives we don't want others to see. No one posts about their deepest hardships on Facebook or Instagram. At least, no one I know. We post the parts of ourselves we feel good about.

We can't compare ourselves to those around us. We're all different in our own unique ways, and that's something to be celebrated!

Secondly, practice gratitude. What are you grateful for? Before you say "nothing," really consider what it means to be grateful. Gratitude comes from satisfaction and acknowledgment; it's the process of looking at the world and saying, "this is pretty cool."

So what makes you feel grateful? Is it sunny days, your family, supportive friends, a great workout, or a certain hobby? Maybe you're grateful for a season, your pet, or a piece of furniture.

For example, I'm grateful for the adorable rug I found on Etsy. I spent months looking for deals, and I finally found a piece I loved! This is a small example, but I'm grateful for the hard work and time someone put into weaving the rug and the time I put into finding it. Consider what you're grateful for every day. You don't need to write things down, though many people find that helpful. I keep a gratitude journal and spend five minutes a day thinking about what I'm grateful for. The list can be relatively short at first; I started with just three or four bullets. Over time, my lists grew pretty long!

Next, consider how you work through stress. This one might seem a little odd or maybe even confusing, so I'll spell it out for you!

When you experience a negative or stressful event, how do you cope? Do you push it away, focus elsewhere, and neglect your feelings? If so, you're not alone. Most people have a difficult time facing negative, stressful occurrences. That's alright!

Look at things head-on when they don't go your way. Write down your feelings, meditate, or practice mindfulness. Think to yourself, "This is what's happening, this is how I feel about it, and this is how I can get through it."

Use the tools at your disposal to work through times of difficulty.

Lastly, happiness is infectious. Think about the happy people in your life. Most people like being around happy people; we're drawn to them and we admire them. What do happy people do? They smile, give thoughtful compliments, and maintain their cool in the face of crisis or hardship.

Try smiling at the gardener outside your building. Hold the door open for the woman with hands full of groceries. Thank the attendant at the grocery store. Thank everyone!

When we give happiness, we get happiness.

Your Future With Happiness

You deserve happiness. You deserve a better life. You deserve a future worth living.

There's no formula or secret hack to happiness. Like anything else in life, we have to work for it. If you're not happy with a certain aspect of your life (you don't like your job, your partner is on your back, or your apartment is messy), you have the chance to change it.

Your happiness isn't determined by your circumstances. There are people of all income levels, education levels, and life stages who feel happy. Happiness comes from the person you see in the mirror.

Choose happiness today.

Chapter 6—Create Everyday

What do you think of when you think of the word "creativity?" Do you think of art, music, writing, etc? Those activities require creativity, but creativity goes far beyond putting words on a page or coming up with a catchy tune.

Creativity is the process of generating new ideas and concepts. It's how we express our ideas and feelings. Engineers use creativity just as painters do. It's the same thought process!

Have you heard the phrase, "I guess I'm just not creative," or, "I'm not an artistic person." Guess what? That's a myth. We are all born with the ability to be creative. Creativity is like athleticism: Some people are inherently better at sports, but we can all learn to run a mile with enough training.

Experts say all children are born with a certain level of creativity, but we lose that creativity during adulthood. As we get older, creativity becomes a bit of an afterthought. You're bombarded with responsibilities, habits, and things ' to do,' so why bother exercising your creative muscles?

While it takes time, it's ultimately worth it.

There are different types of creativity, so we won't go too far into each one. Consider what you do each day that's a little creative. Maybe you take a new route to work or find a 'hack' to make a better cup of coffee. Maybe you journal, write or find a new method of cooking dinner.

All of these are ways we express our creativity. You have it in you, but sometimes we need a little guidance.

Creativity and Uniqueness

As we age, we lose creative focus. Ideas become ingrained, habits are reinforced, and laundry and food take precedence over ingenuity. It happens, but it doesn't necessarily have to.

I'm by no means saying you have to forego paying bills or picking your children up for school to paint for a while, I'm saying it's high time to unlock who you are and express it.

Creativity is the habit of expressing your uniqueness. What makes you, you? What do you enjoy? What topics do you find especially compelling? What do you notice about the world around you?

I was in a Taco Bell drive thru, looked down and saw these leaves. The sun hit the water drops and the leaf colors were autumn-perfection. I stepped out of my car and snapped this picture. Later that night, I saw a talented friend who wrote a Haiku and it was published! That led me to try and write a poem. One act of noticing the beauty around me, led to another of trying to write a poem about the picture. It doesn't matter if your creativity leads to a product - it just matters that you exercise your creativity muscle and feel that rush of endorphins!

perfect Fall leaves
meditate water drop

What you say, how you say it, and what you do comes from you. That's creativity at its finest!

Creativity and confidence go hand in hand; when we engage with our creative ideas, and share them, we gain confidence in ourselves.

Think about the last time you found a creative solution to a problem. Let's say you're invited to a potluck dinner party, and you decide to make your mother's lasagna recipe. You walk over to the pantry, only to find you forgot to buy red sauce! You've already raved about the recipe, and two friends messaged you to tell you how excited they were!

Shoot—what's next?

You decide to find a creative solution to the problem. You scrounge up some tomatoes from the back of your fridge, and they look okay, so you check out "make your own pasta sauce" articles. You add the ingredients together, and boom! You have a small taste before starting the rest of the recipe, and the sauce is delicious!

Not only can you brag about the entire recipe being made from scratch, but you feel pretty good about yourself, right?

Finding new ways to do a certain task or conquer a roadblock brings us creativity. And oddly, enough, the same concept applies to time management. When we find a creative way to do a task or solve a problem, it comes much easier and we feel better doing it!

Daydream

Think back to when you were in school. Did you ever look out the window in the middle of class and let your mind drift off into an idea, concept, or feeling? Maybe you were thinking about a problem or what you wanted to do in the future. If this resonates with you,

you're not alone; I did it too! I may have even forgotten I was actually playing in a softball game until the ball sailed over my head. Oops!

Daydreaming isn't a bad thing. We're taught not to daydream (stay focused, my teacher always said), but there's nothing wrong with letting your mind get lost in a concept or idea for a little while, at least, at an appropriate time.

Daydreaming and being distracted aren't the same thing. You're surrounded by possible distractions right now! Your phone, cat, bookshelf, or family are all distractions. Daydreaming is different—daydreaming is the process of letting your mind do the work, leaving other forms of stimuli by the wayside. They're two completely different things!

Daydreaming spurs creativity, intelligence, and conceptual awareness. I'm not saying you should daydream while driving home; I'm saying it's important to let your brain take you to an idea or problem that's been on your mind.

Take a few minutes each day to daydream. Sit on your bed, in a comfy chair, or another safe space, and let yourself get lost. If you need a little inspiration, try reading a book for a bit or listening to music!

Daydreaming is a great way to get started with creativity. Give it a try!

Use Nature

Before you roll your eyes, hear me out—nature is a great way to explore what's around you and spur your creativity. Not only is it low-cost (or free), it's engaging!

Try walking around your local park or neighborhood. If you live in a large city, no worries! Walking around the city is another great way to start tapping into what your mind has to offer.

When you're exploring nature, ask yourself these questions:

- What am I seeing?
- Who is around me?
- What sounds do I hear?
- What about colors?
- How are others engaging with their surroundings?

Feel free to take photos and notes, or just soak in what the world around you has to offer. Not only will you get your body's muscles moving, but you'll also get your brain muscles warmed up too.

Explore Your Boundaries

We tend to get stuck in our ways. However, I encourage you to try things that make you a little uncomfortable. Explore an area you normally wouldn't or head out for a walk if it's been a while. (Of course, safety always comes first.) Make a new recipe using flavors you haven't tried, or call up an acquaintance.

Exploring your boundaries gives you a better sense of what life has to offer. And not only that, it gives you a sense of confidence! You might find you're not a huge fan of the new flavors you tried in last night's dinner, and that's okay! You learned something entirely new.

Trying new things gives us control and expands our minds. If you don't like something, don't do it again! But if you do, keep exploring!

Easy Ways to Expand Your Creative Mind

We've talked about a few ways to get the juices flowing, so now it's time to put what you've learned into action! Don't feel stupid or silly. Many creative techniques seem mundane or childish, but children are inherently creative; maybe they're onto something.

I have a colleague who loves having beautiful fingernails. Every two weeks, she visits the nail salon for a manicure. This always involves diving into her nail art Pinterest board. It might seem silly (I didn't get it at first), but it counts! Whatever suits your fancy.

We've gone over a long list of things you can do to feel more creative and exercise your mind. Give them a try.

- Draw for a while. You don't need to be an artist or comic; sit down with a pencil and paper and sketch something around you: a chair, a plant, or even mimic a piece of artwork!

- Write something. Again, you don't have to be J.K. Rowling or John Grisham to give writing a try. Sit at a desk and journal or practice writing a short story. You might write about a past event or about something you hope to happen in the future.

- Give knitting or crocheting a try! I was skeptical about knitting for a while, but I found repetitive tasks give me peace and a sense of calm. And on top of that, I've finally nailed the purl stitch! Knitting or crocheting is a great (and cost-effective) way to release tension.

- Go outside and garden. This might not be an option for everyone, but if you have a bit of space and some time, there's nothing stopping you!

- Listen to music. You've likely heard this one before, but it's a fantastic, and again, low-cost, way to expand your mind. Try listening to a genre you normally don't. I'm an 80s music fan myself, but I've grown fond of newer pop songs.

- Do a brain game like Sudoku, crossword puzzle or Solitaire. Not only are you exercising your creativity, but you're giving your brain a boost!

- Learn about something new, even if it seems a little nerdy. I was a bit of a nerd (100% nerd) growing up—I loved European History! It sounds lame, but I still listen to interesting documentaries about early England. Learn about what compels you and makes you think. Draw connections!

These are just a few examples. If you don't find any of these ideas interesting, look up others. You're responsible for yourself, and it's your job to better your life. You're in control.

Your Creative Future

Creativity is the process we use to solve problems, explore what makes us unique, and realize what's around us.

Most recently, I bought myself a set of magnetic poetry words and put them on my fridge. Each morning I rearrange the words into a short poem about what I'm feeling or thinking. I'm no poet, but it makes me feel a little creative. I'm not kidding! You'll feel a sense of fulfillment.

Let's try an exercise together.

How many words can be made out of the letters in the word: CHRISTMAS?
A. 25
B. 75
C. 125
D. 300

Try writing down some words using those letters. Mast, masts, his, mist, chasm—I could go on forever.

Believe it or not, you can actually make over 300 words using only the letters in Christmas.

After that, add "Merry" to "Christmas" and you can come up with over 1,300 words!

Creativity isn't out of reach; you're born a creative. Creativity can be exercised, just like a muscle. And, more importantly, creativity is something you can share with others! It's like a little bonus.

When I took up knitting, I began making little potholders and scarves for my friends as gifts! While they didn't always look professional, I felt better giving someone something I'd made myself. Most recently, I gave an old co-worker some potholders as a housewarming gift. They ended up holding a dinner party for some new friends, and sent me photos of them using the potholders!

Watching people enjoy your creativity is rewarding. I feel the same satisfaction when I read book reviews after I release the project! A warm grin washes over my face when someone writes "I've started a great new morning routine!" after reading my book, *The Shower Habit.*

I felt like a confident badass!

You can do it too; creativity is within all of us.

Note from Stephanie

While you are in a creative mood, would you consider going to Amazon and leaving a review? I am still very much a fledgling author, and reviews help so much. Thank you! And remember to go to StephanieEwingAuthor.com to pick up your free extras to boost your success!

Tip Two
Great Reads

You Are A Badass by Jen Sincero
Atomic Habits by James Clear
The Miracle Morning by Hal Elrod
The Total Money Makeover
by Dave Ramsey
The 4-Hour Work Week
by Timothy Ferriss
The Checklist Manifesto
by Atul Gawande
The Five Second Rule by Mel Robbins

Check out this book by Stephanie Ewing on Amazon now.

Chapter 7—Value of Reading

It's confession time. I feel most creative, engaged, and focused while listening to nonfiction audiobooks. Is that a little odd or weird? Maybe. To me, reading, and reading often is a means of spurring my creativity, learning new things, and energizing my mind.

This might seem like a bit of a plug—I'm a nonfiction writer, but I was a reader and word geek long before I picked up a pen and paper. While I have a certain affinity for writing, I began as a reader, hunched in my childhood bedroom over the books my parents kept on their bookshelf.

To me, reading is a jolt of caffeine to my brain; it kickstarts my idea mill and everything seems to fall into place. I read both fiction and nonfiction. I might sound a little like your high school English teacher—the one who told you *Moby Dick* was a must-read and preached the value of reading for hours on end. While I hold my personal biases about reading, I speak to you as a friend. Reading more is an easy, cost-effective tool to change your outlook.

Let's dive into it.

The Benefits of Reading

You might not believe me yet, and that's okay. If not, I'm here to convince you. In this section, we'll discuss a few of the many benefits of reading more, and reading often. Reading includes listening to audiobooks.

Quell Your Stress

To many, reading seems like a time waster, or a luxury we simply can't afford. Guess what? We can't afford not to.

Reading allows you to slow down and focus solely on what's in front of you. It's a means of opening your mind and reducing stress. It's much different than watching a movie or TV show. When we watch TV, we're shown what the director wants us to see. The images are right there in front of you in shapes and colors. While I love TV as much as the next person, I'll be the first to say that it doesn't spur my creativity or lower my stress levels as much as reading.

Reading asks the reader to use their imagination. You aren't shown an image; you create an image. Readers put pieces together and enlist their brains to guide them through the page. It's repetitive, calming, and methodic.

Certain studies show a link between stress reduction and reading on a cognitive level. On average, reading reduces stress and anxiety by nearly 70%, making it a pretty effective way to release your worries.

Many people read on vacation. I love sitting on a beach when I get the chance to do so and enjoying a book while soaking in the sun. It's relaxing—if it weren't, I wouldn't do it during my precious vacation time!

Reading & The Mind

Reading is calming, but can it actually make you smarter? The short answer is yes.

Reading engages your memory and cognition. Think about it this way: While you read, you're forced to retain information and synthesize it to put together a plot. The characters' names repeat, their actions are referred to repeatedly, and the facts come together to help you understand what the book is about.

The process of remembering what's happening in a book jumpstarts our memory, just like a word puzzle or a game of Sudoku. Let's say you sit down and read a chapter at a time—there are 10 chapters in the book you're reading, and each one builds off of the one before. When you pick up the book at Chapter 4, you're forced to remember what happened in Chapter 3 and the ones prior.

As humans, we often find ourselves becoming a bit forgetful. I'm no stranger to this idea. I forget dates, deadlines, and tasks, only to lay in bed at night and think, "Crap, that's what I was supposed to do today!" It's an unwelcome panicky feeling, and I sure don't like it.

When we read, our brain exercises the skills necessary to remember what's going on. Those who read find themselves less forgetful than their non-reading counterparts.

The benefits go beyond memory—those who read might improve their cognition long term. Experts believe that reading can delay or subvert the onset of degenerative neurological diseases like dementia. Readers enjoy improved mood, creativity, and memory.

Reading and Emotions

Think about your favorite celebrity, TV show, or book. How do you feel about the characters? Do you become attached to them? I certainly do!

I was a huge *Bones* fan, and without dropping any spoilers, I felt personally victimized when certain characters left the show.

Reading works the same way, even if you're reading nonfiction. Nonfiction stories are often rooted in 'characters,' the only difference being that the characters and events really happened. We feel for the characters; we love them; we want them to succeed.

When we read, we become fully immersed in what's happening on the page. We understand the characters and visualize them. We often see parts of ourselves in the characters, which only makes them more real. It's those connections that improve our emotional intelligence and empathy.

Nonfiction and Vocabulary: The Intelligence Hack

Reading enhances your vocabulary and writing skills—that's simply a fact. But what about spelling and perception? How does that play a role in the reading process?

When I was younger I enrolled in my middle school's spelling bee. I was a pretty good speller and I really wanted to win. Do you know what my teacher told me? She said, "Read more."

Don't just take it from me; experts say that reading is one of the best ways to improve spelling and vocabulary. It's a key marker between those with strong vocabularies and those who become stuck on words.

We're more likely to perceive others as intelligent if they use formal and accurate vocabulary. The same concept applies to you!

Nonfiction teaches you new things and ways of thinking. You're learning new facts, concepts, and ways of life. These facts reinforce your thoughts and perceptions, allowing you to draw new connections about the world around you. It's like a class, except you're teaching yourself!

How to Read More Often

Well, it comes down to time management. Time management is a common theme throughout this book. Ultimately, we make time for what's important to us; we prioritize, engage, and interact with what we like or what must be done. It's unlikely you make time for things you find silly, small, or unimportant. When you're faced with a deadline, the task becomes a priority. But if not, or if you don't particularly like something, it's not at the top of your to-do list.

You don't have to waste your time reading things you find dry or boring. The best writers and the best books frame arguments and hard-to-reach concepts in a way readers find interesting. Any type of nonfiction will work as long as you find it interesting.

Think back to the "Start Small" chapter. Don't dive into reading all at once. If it's been years since you've cracked a book, it would be unreasonable to think you can read one from start to finish in one sitting.

Start by reading one chapter, article, or blog a day. Don't read for longer than fifteen minutes. Of course, if you find the material particularly cool, let yourself read a bit longer. If not, try setting a timer and, when it dings, you're done for the day. Little reading spurts allow you to learn a lot over time.

Reading doesn't have to break the bank either. Many books are available used or at a low cost on Amazon, and feel free to use your local library to find nonfiction books you find interesting. Don't hesitate to reach out to a friend. I have a "reader" friend who lends me books each month.

Learn to make time for reading. Reading every day doesn't have to involve sitting down in a perfectly quiet, well-lit space; for most of us, that's just a fever dream. You can read blogs, biographies, articles, self-help books (hint!), or pretty much whatever you like!

Chapter 8—Post-It Notes

Begin what I call the post-it habit. At the end of each day, write down the things you'd like to accomplish the next. It doesn't matter what you write down, as long as it's important to you.

Here are a few examples:
- Get 10,000 steps at the gym, around your neighborhood, or in your house
- Write 1,000 words in a journal or book
- Eat more veggies (preferably green ones)
- Drink one cup of coffee. If you're a caffeine addict like me, try drinking less coffee in smaller increments.
- Smile more. This is a common one, and we briefly discussed it in the earlier chapters. It works, y'all.
- Hold the door open for someone, whether it be at work, school, the grocery store, etc!
- Go to the gym, just for 20 minutes.
- Finish the laundry you've been putting off.
- Make a budget for next month.

Again, it doesn't matter what you write down, as long as it's important, timely, and measurable. Don't write "be happy," or "get things done." Those aren't measurable habits. The goal is for you to see the work you've put in and to cross things off your list.

Once you're finished with the list for the night, put the post-it note on a surface you can clearly see, like your coffee maker, front door, or by your desk. The next day, take it with you, whether it be in your pocket, purse, or coat jacket. It doesn't matter, but you must remember what you've written. That way, you can apply it and master your daily tasks!

Remember, this is your benchmark; the post-it is your goal. You're an accomplished person who can succeed. It's well within you.

You might consider adding "I am successful," to your personal mantra. I repeat this statement in the shower almost every morning. It's not a lie; read your post-it note and feel that sense of accomplishment

Breaking Through the Ordinary

Most recently I listened to Stephen King's *On Writing: The Memoir of the Craft.* Stephen King is kind of a weird dude—he's dealt with more than his fair share of demons (in real life and on paper), but he's a genius. At the end of the audiobook, he includes a speaking event he attended with his son.

One of the main questions he asks and answers is about doubting your work, otherwise known as imposter syndrome. Stephen King, no matter how famous or lauded he is, experiences doubt every time he writes. He's published over 200 novels, and many went on to become bestsellers, but he still experiences doubt and anguish when he sits down to type.

Nevertheless, he puts on his big boy pants and works through his worries just like you and I.

The more you read and learn about your idols, the ones you admire and adore, the more you learn simply how ordinary they are. Their problems are just like yours, whether they're working through love, relationship difficulties, work blunders, and mental health issues.

And, the more we read about "ordinary" people, the more we come to realize the heroism within the ordinary. There's no hubris in saying that you can learn something from everyone.

Many seemingly "ordinary" people cope with anxiety, depression, sobriety, weight loss issues, illness, cancer diagnoses, or work troubles. These are the unseen struggles that reside within the "ordinary." Some days you might feel the burden is insurmountable, like rolling a rock up a hill, but we all carry this individual baggage in some way or another. You're certainly in good company.

Some people have already figured out how to use this baggage: They put it on wheels so to speak, and pulling it around seems effortless for them. Newsflash—it wasn't always a breeze.

I've experienced unimaginable success in my life. I have two beautiful children, a loving partner, a strong, united family, and a career I love and value. But it wasn't always this way. I battled breast cancer a few years ago. But my partner and I worked hard, listened to Dave Ramsey, and bought great real estate purchases. I'm debt-free and own three homes, which I think is a feat in and of itself.

I'm still a self-proclaimed reformed procrastinator. I know myself, perhaps all too well, and know I need deadlines or I just fizzle out. I consider myself a driven person, but I experience attention-deficit detours more often than I care to admit. I'm passionate, but often forget to see the entire forest or the blue sky above, and instead focus on a few leaves or gray clouds.

I go to see my oncologist every six months, and it's always a glaring reminder of my own mortality. I experience fear, procrastination, anxiety, and self-doubt just like everyone else, but I've learned some fun and (mostly) healthy ways to cope with what life hands me.

I go for frequent walks, enjoy photography, pet my cats or dogs, get a massage, enjoy a long hug from a dear friend or loved one, set short-term and long-term goals, celebrate small wins, give gifts, laugh over chips and margaritas with friends. I love these activities; they fill my bucket and keep me movin' right along.

So what fills your bucket? What activities do you enjoy? You might think "nothing really," but that can't be true! Everyone has something that piques their interest. Do you enjoy exercise, time with friends or family, or taking naps (you're not alone there)? Do you enjoy movies, music, or TV? Maybe pottery, knitting, painting, or journaling are your coping-skill drinks of choice.

Regardless of what makes you feel fulfilled, there's something. Making time for that something is just as important as making time for dinner or errands. You come first, at least some of the time!

Chapter 9—START

Emergence: In philosophy, systems theory, science, and art, emergence occurs when an entity is observed to have properties its parts do not have on their own, properties or behaviors that emerge only when the parts interact in a wider whole. Emergence plays a central role in theories of integrative levels and of complex systems.

You're capable of making your own change, and more importantly, it's time to get started. We covered a lot of information in this book, but ultimately I want you to think about how you can incorporate these ideas into your own life.

Ask yourself:

- What am I sacrificing by procrastinating?
- Am I satisfied with my life right now?
- What am I missing?
- What can I change? What can't I change?
- Am I using my creativity to tackle negative events?
- Am I using the tools and skills I have to become a better person?
- Am I sharing my gifts or passion with the world?

Where would you like to be in five years? Would you like to take on a more hands-on position at work? Would you like to have a family? Are you interested in moving? Really sit down and think about your future. How can you get there?

Tell the part of your brain that repeats, "I'm not worthy" to shut the f**k up! It's not serving you.

Say it with me:
I am strong.
I am successful.
I accomplish my goals.

Note from the Author

I greatly appreciate your time reading this book. I hope you have nailed down your procrastination type and figure out a way around it. I believe in you!

I would absolutely love it if you would take a few minutes to leave a review on Amazon. I want to help as many people as possible achieve healthy habits. Reviews help this book reach more readers. I would also really like to hear your questions or comments. Your honesty will help me write even better books for you.
Thank you,
Stephanie

Tip Three
You Got This

"People who are crazy enough to think they can change the world, are the ones who do."
– *Steve Jobs*

"A ship in harbor is safe, but that is not what ships are built for."
– *John A. Shedd*

"When everything seems to be going against you, remember that the airplane takes off against the wind, not with it."
– *Henry Ford*